T0068089

The Soul Of The Black Butterfly

RASHEEDA J. STEWARD

To learn more about this Author visit her at:
www.thealabasterhouse.org / www.agodconnector.org
Always, Always Stay Prayerful

authorHOUSE®

AuthorHouse™
1663 Liberty Drive
Bloomington, IN 47403
www.authorhouse.com
Phone: 1-800-839-8640

© *2005 by Rasheeda J. Steward. All rights reserved.*

No part of this book may be reproduced, stored in a retrieval system, or transmitted by any means without the written permission of the author.

Published by AuthorHouse   10/18/2012

ISBN: 978-1-4772-0488-7 (sc)
ISBN: 978-1-4772-0469-6 (e)

Library of Congress Control Number: 2012908592

Any people depicted in stock imagery provided by Thinkstock are models, and such images are being used for illustrative purposes only.
Certain stock imagery © Thinkstock.

This book is printed on acid-free paper.

Because of the dynamic nature of the Internet, any web addresses or links contained in this book may have changed since publication and may no longer be valid. The views expressed in this work are solely those of the author and do not necessarily reflect the views of the publisher, and the publisher hereby disclaims any responsibility for them.

dedicate this book to All, ALL Those I LOVE
In every Poem there is a part of me and a part of you… Truly
You ARE my greatest Inspiration

I Love You Mom & Thanks for loving me back

Special thanks to Artist Cheryl Butler for the portrait of
The Black Butterfly

Thank you Lord for the cords that have been AND will be broken
To God Be the Glory

About the Author

This author, as many women, wears many hats. Her hats of mothering, teaching, and nursing melded; is the unction for her most notable hat: "Minister of God's-Love." For 35 years, Rasheeda has strived to perfect her walk with Christ. In doing so, she has concluded: "Serving in Faith; with the unconditional Love of God," is a true Christian's walk. Her salvation is not a religion; her relationship with God is not hard; it is her way of life. To God be the Glory . . .

Her given name (Henrietta AJ Steward) did not depict who she was. With God's guidance, through many challenging, metamorphic trials and tribulations, she has found her place in life. Unbeknown to her, God had already ordained who she was. In 1985, she was enlightened to her God-given name and her life's purpose. Rasheeda: *One of Wisdom, a Righteous Guide, and an Angel.* Aka: Lady-Brown, she became Founder and President of a nonprofit Out-Reach-Organization: *God's Connectors Inc.*, where God has shown her, her ability to serve and teach others. Yes, an Angel she has been to many while *connecting them to God's out stretched hand.*

Incredibly as it is, while she had been an angel to many; this wingless angel was broken. Like a broken winged butterfly, that had been pulled from its cocoon too soon, she felt destined to never fly. She lived years in a dark cocoon while in *God's-hovering-Grace*, where she studied the word of God and herself, receiving healing from life's hurts and Victory-Over-People. Finally, the Divine-Healing of her wings came in the summer of 2010. Now, she looks forward to soaring higher <u>in God's Love everyday!</u>

This Book of Psalms is her story. As you read she promises Enjoyment, Comfort, Hope, Peace, Increased Faith, perhaps a little tear shedding; but for sure enlightenment into your own Butterfly Soul.

Contents

Today's Future

**And Jesus said unto him,
Verily I say unto thee;
Today shalt thou be with me in paradise
Luke 23:43**

Yesterday will never become Tomorrow
As Tomorrow comes, Today appears
Your future has begun
With the rising of the sun

So live Today as you would Tomorrow
Then you will never look back
With Yesterday's sorrows

Your future is destined Today
What it will become on Tomorrow
Don't hinder it by what you didn't do Yesterday
While waiting for a future dollar
Or for another to holler
You have the power today to lead your way
And even another that's tempted to stray

Your Future is Today

Live It as you dream for tomorrow

The Boxed

Now therefore, if ye will obey my voice indeed, and
Keep my covenant, then ye shall be a peculiar treasure
Unto me above all people: for all the earth is mine:
Exodus 19:5

Have you ever wondered why it seems
That some people's lives are extreme
While others are content to only breathe
And swallow more food than they need

Look around and see
Some people seem to be stuck on life's tree
Their past has engulfed them in while time has moved on
But they don't seem to extend nor move beyond the norm

Their Hopes and Dreams are only an arm reach away
Yet their goals have not been achieved
Some think they will never be a Jewel of the most high King
They are boxed with fear and not set free

Some live in this box struggling to get out
While these seem content being boxed about
Time, Faith and Hope as we know
Is life's key to the "treasure box" the Master holds

Though life may be unkind
You are a Precious Jewel that will show in its time
You must see from beneath life's incidental 'stuff'
The Diamond you are in the rough
Some strive and many fail
For no one has told them they are
The Pearl in an oyster shell

The Boxed

It is sad to say but it is true
Only a few have realized
They have not been shaped to be confined in a cube
Their dreams are too wide, their hopes are too high
Their love for life is much too deep
Their faith in God is too strong
And they will not be kept weak

These must be freed from the box
From the walls of life that attempts
To hold them as a caged fox

These have made up their minds
They will not be trapped or bind
Their spirit longs to be set free
To swore and run to feel the wind's breeze
To reach their widest dream
To go beyond their highest hope
These would never be found confined to dope

These will excel, yes these will fly high
And one day go beyond the sky
These are those who will never remain boxed or tied
For these are the Master's Precious Jewels
Prepared for the Master's mighty uses

A Wrong Turn

Thou hast set a bound that they
may not pass over; that they
turn not again to cover the earth.
Psalm 104:9

Have you ever been traveling going towards a direct destination
Somehow in a blink of an eye you found you were lost in the wrong
location

What happened, you read the signs, you followed the map
You opened the window, played the music and even snacked in order
not to nap

You have gone where you weren't called to go
Now all around you is changed from that you know

Hopes and dreams have come to a halt
In a tangled web you seem to be caught

Now you cry, How, how do I get back on track
BUT Pride and time won't let you turn back

What, what went wrong
You thought you were ready and strong

You went in the direction of your mind
You failed to follow that which was inside

A Wrong Turn

Detours, dead ends and dark winding roads have all left you in a
spin

Quietly the question haunts you from within
How long will it take to get your life on the right path again

One wrong turn has left you lost, alone and in a state of confusion
The road you chose you see now was only a delusion

No matter how cautious of a step one might make
Somehow, somewhere the wrong turn we are liable to take

This is true when We try to choose what path is best
But if we TRUST in the Lord He will order our steps

Rather He allows the scenic route
Or a long dark tunnel God will guide you out

He will turn you around
Even now if you're not too proud to let your knees hit the ground

Do you know the Lord God yearns
To help you find your "Right Turn"

"God Don't Lie"

God is not a man, that He should lie;
Neither the son of man that He should repent:
Hath He said, and shall He not do it?
Or hath He spoken, and shall He not make it good?
Numbers 23:19

The Lord has recompensed my evil with good
He has taken me from the 'valley of low'
Just as he said He could
The journey's been long but He promised he would

Never lose your expectation
Keep your confidence in all situations
Walk in divine 'Righteousness' and
Your promise will come with total happiness

God is not a God that He should lie
Just trust Him and see by and by
It may seem slow
But if God said it, it will be so

That which you wait for will come to pass
Your valley experience won't forever last

Even that which your enemy meant for bad
The Lord will use it to build you and make you glad
Though all looks dark and you honestly can't see your way
Remember it is true "trouble don't last always

God Don't Lie

Hold on and keep your faith
Joy is coming with a brand new day

You say; life has been unfair
You have gotten to the point where you really don't care
Know for sure God has not given you a spirit of doubt or fear
He will make you strong just keep your mind clear

God is not a God that He should lie
Just trust Him, wait and you will see by and by
It may seem slow
But know if God said it, it is so

That which you wait for will come to pass
Your valley experience won't forever last

Praise Him Now For That You Don't See
GO HEAD Confuse Your Enemy . . .

Does He Really Care

Out of the depths have I cried unto thee, O Lord.
Lord, hear my voice: let thine ears be attentive to
The voice of my supplications.
Psalm 130:1-2

Where is Jesus when all goes wrong
He promised to never leave us along
Yet No matter how much you trust in God's shinning light
There are times in life
When nothing seems to go right

We walk by faith and not by sight
The battle is won but yet we fight
Yes there are times when our faith is dim
The war that we face is depressing and grim

When all hell is breaking loose in our life
Where is God with the Victory from the fight
We stand on God's statues and His laws
Yet there are times "Murphy" has us against the wall

Lord the troubles that come my way
Causes Your promise from me to fade
Oh God I don't want to doubt or complain
I know Your hand is present or else
I would have already gone insane

Beyond any dispute
I know Lord You really do care
Your hand unseen is visible everywhere
So Please strengthen my eyes to see
Your already made path for me

So the question is not for you to choose
You Can See, Yes
God Really Does Care for you???

Even when life seems unfair
Sometimes there are things He must tear
down, away, apart and pluck from our heart
Only because He Really Does Care
Remember He died to set you free
From tomorrow's misery

I love You Divinely

I am persuaded, that neither death, nor life,
Nor angels, nor principalities, nor powers,
Nor things present, nor things to come,
Nor, height, nor depth, nor any other creature,
Shall be able to separate us from the love of God,
Which is in Christ Jesus our Lord.
Rom.8:38-39

Oh Precious Lord, You have made me divinely
To Serve You, to Praise you, to Worship you
To Love You till the end of time
Why then should I sit and cry
Because "so-called-friends" say good-bye
They leave me in the night
When wrong is no longer right

You My Lord paid the cost
To keep me from being eternally lost
I know You will never Leave me
Forsake me or bind me in fear
But You will always be there

So I praise you, I worship You
I love You divinely

My Lord have promised . . .
To comfort me, console me, to hold me
always to guide me . . .
To be by my side, to protect me and to find me
If my path I should stray
By a hand that pulls me away
I know your love for me will not fade

That's why I praise you, I worship you
I love you divinely

Why should I waste time to fraught
Because something from me they don't get
I know Dear Lord Your way is right
I can not compromise in the night
You are my friend and You have not failed me yet
So I will continue to Praise You
Worship You and Love you divinely

I love You Divinely

Who can come against me to cause me to be afraid
No weapon formed will make me give in to their way
I know My Lord You will hide me
In the shadow of your loving wings
There You will make me strong so I will always sing
Praise to You and worship in song
For you I love and divinely to you I belong

So I Praise You, I Worship You and I will Love You till all time
For You have made me and that so Divine

"The Potter's Mended Vessel"

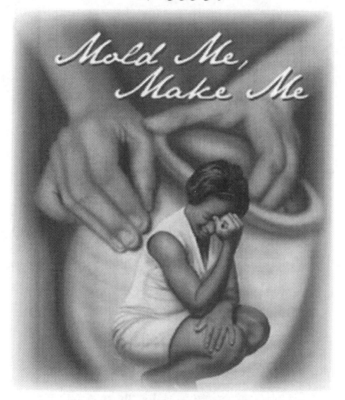

Mold Me, Make Me

And the vessel that he made of clay
Was marred in the hand of the potter:
So he made it again another vessel,
As seemed good to the potter to make it.
Jeremiah 18:4

Here again on the Potter's wheel
Should I be sad or should I be thrilled
What lesson for me awaits
I know my destination I won't escape

In the heat I know I must bake
There trials, struggles, temptations and fears
Will test my growing faith
The Potter exams the broken vessel in hand
His tender touch restores
He enables it to stand

Oh Master the fire is much too hot
What lesson is it I have not yet got
I am thine vessel made with thine own hand
Teach me Master not to pull from thine plan

Round and around and round I go
It's all to strengthen me, yes I know
I want to be that vessel filled for thine Glory
Able to stand strong to tell Your heavenly story

The Potter's Mended Vessel

From the wheel to the fire
I know He is making me worthy
And taking me higher
When it all feels a bit too much
He comforts me with a gentle touch
In the oven again I bake
How much more heat Master must I take

On the shelf the Vessel now stands
Ready to hear the Master's every command
The potter is proud and glorified
For the vessel is mended and more purified
A vessel of honor to magnify

The Potter's handy work surely has been tried
But now with gratification the Vessel has stood its test of time
Look at the Praising vessel how it shines
The Potter is pleased with the Vessel He holds
It's taken awhile but now the Master is in full control

I Praise My Lord, for loving me enough
To place me on the wheel of his loving touch
Here I am again
Amen & Amen

Looking For The Answer

**I will lift up mine eyes unto the hills,
from whence cometh my help.
Psalms 121:1**

When life becomes a mystery
Where does the answer lie?
When your soul longs to be set free
Where does the answer lie?

When all your dreams seem so far away
Where does the answer lie?
When all you can do is hope and pray
Where does the answer lie?

When your yesterday becomes your today
Where does the answer lie?
As you watch your tomorrow fade away
Where does the answer lie?
When you have done all you can
Where does the answer lie
With no reward you continue to stand
Where does the answer lie

Look, look inside
It is there in your heart
Listen, listen to the one who is not so far
If you listen you will hear
If you look you will see
You have the answer and the key
Where does the answer lie

The Answer is not lost
But only when you are found
Will you know where to look
For the Answer is alive and not bound

So go within
Find your strength
And unlock the answers
Given

"My Comforter Is You"

For the Lord shall comfort Zion: He will comfort
All her waste places; and he will make her wilderness
Like Eden, and her desert like the garden of the Lord;
Joy and gladness shall be found therein, thanksgiving,
And the voice of melody.
Isaiah 51:3

So many times I have carried my own Load
I have failed to come to you humbly and bold
You have told me "bring me your burdens and cares"
Yet it has been so hard for me to leave them there

I have heard the truth all my life
Words of wisdom has kept me from strife
Though now I sit where I cannot move
Because I failed to see the right path to choose

Comfort I now need and cannot find
There's no hand of love no one here is kind
Oh my God!! How I miss all that was free
I long for the Love and comfort that was given to me

I realize now my Comforter Is You
Only you can carry me through
Help me Lord to dig down deep
To give you all that hinders my peace

There's no one to call, no one to lean
No one around close to being keen
Here I come Lord humble as one can be
My whole load I carry from my knees

Even now, feeling defeat
I will lie in peace and wait on thee
For only you can see me through
For there is nothing no one Nor I can do

My Comforter Is You
And You My Lord
I Know WILL See Me Through

There are times in life we are faced with oppositions and situations
That causes us to feel as if we will lose our ever loving mind
We struggle to hold on by a very thin thread
During these times Jesus is the very Cord
That keeps us connected to the Comfort of God's Peace

. . . Phil 4:7

The Unwatched Sheep

What man of you, having a hundred sheep, if he lose one of them, do not leave the ninety and nine in the wilderness, and go after that which is lost, until he find it? And when he has found it He lays it on his shoulders, rejoicing. Luke 15:4-5

The Shepherd looks over his flock, he counts each sheep
While keeping a watchful eye for the nearby thief
All the sheep are busy eating the fill for the day
The Shepherd scolds with love as one attempts to stray
But wait there is one that seems to be out of place

The Shepherd inquires of the sheep fold
Where that one just might be
Not in the cold? The shepherd pleads

Down at the spring, the word came back
He's getting plenty of water but food he lacks
In darkness he hides where the Light subsides

The watchful Shepherd continues to feed
The attending flock their every need

Though the one down by the stream
For days has not been seen
No one hears him as he cries, kicks and now screams

He waits for his shepherd to come
He listens for the Shepherd's call
Surely this one is loved, as the Shepherd loves them all

The sheep in confusion tries to turn back
Catching his feet in a unseen trap

He waited in expectation to see the Shepherd top the hill
For sure he has to discern what this bemused sheep must feel

The Unwatched Sheep

With tenacity he did what he had been taught
The Shepherd had informed all if ever caught . . .
Down on your knees you must fall and cry . . .
"Give me strength to make it back to the right side"

He instantly heard a voice whisper and say
You belong to Me
I will never leave you alone even when you stray
All you have to do is speak
I Am here to show you My divine way

Man may fail you for the busyness of his day
But you are My sheep even while in the trap you lay

I Am *The Good Shepherd,* you I never will forsake
I Am He who hears you when you *earnestly Pray*

Where Is My Bride

And I John saw the holy city,
New Jerusalem, coming down from God out of heaven,
Prepared as a bride adorned for her husband
Revelation 21: 2

I am ready for My Church where is She?

Where is My Bride
Why is her garment not yet white and purified
There are many wrinkles and blemished sights
She has not yet stood before Me and emptied all from inside

I call her by name everyday
Come to Me let me wipe your tears away
I see the creases in your soul
Let me take you in my arms to console

The flaws the brokenness within
I wait and desire to mend
With just one touch
I the Groom will free you from so much

Where is My Bride
She is not ready to go
There's yet so many she haven't told

I have given the commission to all
My Spirit I have given to those I've called
Go tell the world there is one that wish you to fall
Tell them too, the Groom waits for those
That will prepare for the Master's ball

Where Is My Bride

Where is My Bride
Why is She not ready to go
Too busy with her own affairs
To be bothered with the Father's cares

The Banquet room is set and ready for the Bride
Though it stands empty with only Groom inside

Christ is coming back for His Church real soon
A Church without spot, wrinkle or a blemish
A Church worthy of the honey moon
A Church about Her Father's business
With compassion and holiness
A Church dressed and ready to go

Come on church
Put on your veil, get ready for God's overflow
Come let's go HOME

"Black Velvet"

Who can find a virtuous woman?
For her price is far above rubies.
The heart of husband doth safely trust in her,
So that he shall have no need of spoil.
She will do him good and not evil all the days of her life.
Proverbs 31:10-12

I Am Soft As Black Velvet
Hear Me When I Speak
Strong with a Gentle Touch
Loud yet Very Meek

There Is More to Me Than Meets the Eye
What You Don't See
Would You Recognize

God Has Made Me of Three Parts
Though You Look At Me
Just to Play with My Heart

Have You Even Wondered What Lies In My Soul
No, I'm Not That Deep
Perhaps You Are Just Too Shallow

Yes, I Am Rich as Black Velvet
Hear Me When I Speak
Strong with a Gentle Touch
Loud yet Very Meek

I Am God's Woman A Help Meet Indeed
Here to Hold You Up
Down On My Knees

Why Run From Me Woman of Power
To Be With One Not Meant To Be
Your Significant One In God's *Final* Hour

Yes I am Black and That I Am Proud
I don't mean To be so Strong
Nor To Be Too Loud

Black Velvet

I Am Soft As Black Velvet
Hear Me When I Speak
Strong with a Gentle Touch
Loud yet Very Meek

I Am Your Treasure Sent From Above
Treat Me Accordingly
With Respect and True Love

I Am Not Invisible I Don't Go Away
Though You Only See Me
When You Want To Play

In Your Shadow I Do Stand, Why
Because God has made you the man
Though Together We Can Walk
And Change This Wicked Land

I Am Rich as Black Velvet
Hear Me As I Speak
Strong with a Gentle Touch
Loud yet Very Meek

Black Velvet

My Judas Friend I Will Bend
But I Will Not Brake
The God in My Heart You Will Never Take

I Will Run This Race
With God's Loving Grace

I Will Stand Strong
Even If I Must Stand Alone

For I Am Soft as Black Velvet
Someone Will Hear Me When I Speak

Yes, I Am Strong But I Am Gentle
With God's Divine Touch
I Can Be Firm And Yet Love You Very Much
At Times I May Need To Be a Little Loud
Yet I Am Very Meek
SO
Hear Me When God Speaks . . .

The Great Pretender

Run now, I pray thee, to meet her and say unto her,
Is it well with thee? Is it well with thy husband?
Is it well with the child? And she answered, it is well.
2 King 4:26

Is the smile upon my face a lie or is true
The laughter that escapes from my mouth
Who does it really fool?

Yes, I greet you with a smile
When all the while inside
I hold back the tears I cannot cry

I speak with my mouth that
I will rise above every circumstance
But in my mind I'm afraid
To stand and take a chance

I have doubts and fears no one can see
I speak faith and I say I truly do trust
The one I cannot see beyond life's crust
But at night I lay and I wonder
How will tomorrow truly be

Yes I am the great pretender
What I allow you to see
Is far from my reality

Don't think that I walk
In pretense to fool you to believe a lie
No, it is I that I must convince
I *Will* survive

The Missing Pleasures Of Life

The thief comes not but for to steal, And to kill,
And to destroy; I am come that they might
Have life and that they might have it more abundantly.
St John 10:10

A soft word of encouragement
A smile of intent, eyes of reprimand

Momma's warm loving tender hands
The rattling of Momma's pots and pans

Lying under a full green tree
Enjoying the crisp cool breeze

Alligator shoes and a Rolex too
Enjoying a Saturday convertible drive
With a movie and dinner after the ride

A cold soda sparking on ice
The hot sun beaming down sooo nice

A vanilla ice cream swirled with melted caramel
Hot chocolate and nuts that makes the belly swell

Watching the children swing high
All in play they pretend to fly

A long hot steamy shower
Staying in the bathroom hour after hour

A Saturday nap in the mid afternoon
Hitting that snooze when Monday has come to soon

The Missing Pleasures Of Life

These are just a few pleasures of life
These are the simple pleasures that make life so-o-o right
These are the pleasures we take for granted
Until one day we can no longer be enchanted

These are some pleasures Jesus came to give
He freely paid the price so you and I can live

So for Christ sake
Don't miss the Pleasures of Life
Enjoy them while you are still breathing
Take time and smell the flowers
It is God's will for you to enjoy living
Satan aims to keep you down
He wants you sad, crying and always with a frown
BUT - SMILE
It is OK to live the Promised Abundance of life

"Judge Not"

Thou hypocrite, first cast out the beam
Out of thine own eye; and then shalt thou
See clearly to cast out the mote out of thy
Brother's eye.
Matthew 7:5

You judge me and say my actions
Are sometimes wrong
But I ask
Are you always right?

You judge me even though I strive to be my best
While you think you are "the best"

You judge me while I lend a helping hand to those in need
As you know you could but you turn them away

You judge me for the money in my bank account
But you come to me for a loan

You judge me for being quiet and meek
While you boast aloud in your arrogance

You judge me because I have no *man-given-*"title"
But you hide behind yours and judge while idled

You judge me because I am not perfect
But are you the one that died for God's elect

You judge me because I am not you
Yet you are not me
So how can "you" judge "me"
I don't judge you for being you

Just Pray for me as I pray for you
Only then can God's Love shine through
And He alone will judge me and you
By His Divine hand
He will see us through his perfect plan

Mother's Hand Tells The Story

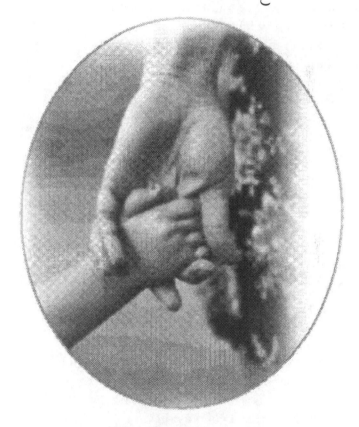

She opens her mouth with wisdom;
and in her tongue is the law of kindness.
She looks well to the ways of her household, and eats
not the bread of idleness.
Her children arise up, and call her blessed; her
husband also, and he praises her.
Proverbs 31: 26-28

A Tender hand a soft touch
Tells you, you are loved ever so much
The hand that reaches out to pull you close to the heart
Tells you there is a Love for you that will never depart

She embraces the child that falls and scrapes his knee
She comforts the one who has faced
Their first day in school with tears and pleads
She gives confidence to her oldest
Who journeys to their very first dance
By one gentle stroke of a Mother's hand
Her children knows it's alright to take a chance

A Mother's hand tells the story
Her hand is strong and firm yet tender and caring

She tells the story with her understanding heart
When life has not been sweet but bitter and tart
Her tender and ever so patient soul is seen
As she bends down to her tired knees
Eye to eye she listens to the concern of her little one
Who pulls consistently at her hem for her to come

Little Johnny knows the story that is told
When she sternly sends him to the corner with a scold
The heart of this loving soul will not tolerate unfair play
But at the end of the day she tells her whole story
With a tender kiss for each child as they lay

A Mother's hand tells the story
Her hand is strong and firm yet tender and caring

No matter what has transpired through the day
A Mother's touch makes it all OK
This is her story, a story of true love
A story that will never end
For her LOVE comes from the One above

"In The 'Mean' Time"

Wait on the Lord: be of good courage,
And He shall strengthen thine heart
Wait, I say, on the Lord.
Psalms 27:14

It is a *mean time doing a time of wait*
It is a time you must stand on your faith
And not be moved from that waiting place

The *mean* time of wait
You will only complicate
If you try to run
From that which is not so fun?

You will be shaken and almost destroyed
But don't you dare faint
Or follow the decoy

It is a *mean* time doing a time of wait
You must stand on your God given faith
And not be moved from that waiting place

Please know this for sure
Your wait only begins
After you have done your hardest chore

Obey the word if you want to receive your reward
The blessings from God will not come
Until you are on one accord

In The 'Mean' Time

In the *mean* time Pray and wait
You must stand and build on your grain of faith
Do not be moved from that waiting place

What a *mean* time to have to wait
Only to find your promise has been delayed
Because you have not yet obeyed

After you have done the will of God
You must now stand and wait
Let patience take her perfect state
It won't be easy but stand in faith
Don't be moved by what you see
Nor let feelings shake you
From what you hope and breathe

It is a *mean* time doing a time of wait
So stand in faith and obey even while you

Wait . . .

Is It Faith 'Or' Is It A Lie?

*Now Faith is the substance of things
Hoped for, the evidence of things not seen
Hebrews 11:1*

There's a thin line between Faith and a Lie
We walk by faith it's not by sight
What we 'feel' we choose not to allow our mind to coincide
What we see we deny is 'not' so
We speak those things that are not as thou they 'show'
We Praise God for that which has not yet manifest
We thank our Lord and we say we are "blessed"
We confess healing while our bodies ache with pain and stress
We believe it is by His strips which has made us whole
Thou we are broken in the pit of our soul
We fight our enemy who's already been defeated
Yet he continues to blind us, bind us and keep us seated
We speak it is by the Blood that has set us free
But the question comes who can be free
In a world such as this we breathe?
We seed the heavens with words of faith to establish earth
Yet the fruit is past it's time of birth

The world looks at us and says we deny the truth and speak only a lie
Though we speak it by faith and in the hope of God that abides
Why should I speak what I don't want to be?
Instead what I say is what I desire to see

So we see faith is not a lie that we speak
It is HOPE in which we live and BELIEVE
By Faith we have the key to invade heaven's door
That negative report don't have to be any more
For if we can receive the TRUTH then all that we speak WILL BE

Is It Faith 'Or' Is It A Lie?

Know that this is No Lie
The words from your mouth controls and binds
By faith you speak what you hope to be
And in God's time it will be–you'll see

It Is Heaven in which we ultimately await by faith
Heaven is our divine destiny that we hope not to escape
But heaven must first start here within our heart
Heaven or Hell it is your choice to be a part
Faith or a Lie the LINE is yours to mark
But one thing I know will never vacate
What you *SPEAK*-Faith *OR* a Lie-becomes yours to take

With your faith in paradise your life will follow

Let's Go To The Other Side

And They came over unto the other side
Of the sea, into the country of the Gardarenes
Mark 5:1

Why have all around me changed
It seems my whole life has been rearranged
That which was once familiar ground
Is now insecure and unsound

I am so unsure about my daily steps
My old path I could have indubitably kept
I felt comfort on yesterday
Today I feel fear along this way

As I kneel and Pray I hear My Lord say
Come let's go to the other side
There I have much more work for you to abide

The other side??!
Here where I stand is fine!
These grounds I have conquered I've even multiplied
The next level I may not swore so high
Elevation brings much responsibilities
Being up high means others will always pull at me
There's no room for mistakes
No time to nullify
Possibly here is my destined place

As I kneel and Pray I hear my Lord say
"Let's go to the other side
I have made you ready to climb another level high
There are deeper depths that you will conquer on that side

There are others that needs to get to the other side
Your doubts and fears not only stops you in your tracks
It will slow and hold others back

On the other side is a better place
On that side in charge you will take

Let's Go To The Other Side

On the other side is unfamiliar ground
Different from any other we together have found
No need to fear standing at the door
Step through it I will lead you as I have many times before"

On my knees I pray once more
Pull me Lord over and up
If I am unsure how to be that needed cup
Forgive me for my unseen fear
I do hear you loud and clear
In you Lord I must be ready
On you I will stand strong and steady

As I stand in relief my soul has emptied it's hidden grief
I will go to the other side where many await as their life collides
I will bring help for all those that stand in hurt
lost in a feeling of being cursed

Thank you Lord for your strength and power
To cross over in this much needed hour

"I Will Wake Up On The Other Side"

My face is foul with weeping,
and on my eyelids is the shadow
of death; Job 16:16

It's morning and the 'Son' is shining bright
Though my eyes are dim I can see His illuminating light
When I close my eyes this time it will all be over at last
My troubles will all be gone my worries will have past

I'll wake up on the other side

My days has been many
My eyes have seen plenty
My pain has been great
My struggles and hurt has been huge
While my accomplishments has been but a few
So much more I wanted to do
So much and now no time
My hands are weak
My eyes are dim
My legs have gone limp
My heart strains to beat without a skip
With pain in the morning straight to noon
All through the night I pray time will be soon

I'll wake up on the other side

They have all gathered around
They've come to fill my heart with last minute joy
Though it's so hard to smile, I try for their heart aches with pain
But I wonder what, what they will do
Once I am gone away
Will they fade from each other
As the sun fades from me

I Will Wake Up On The Other Side

I'll wake up on the other side

How do you say good-bye to those that stand and breathe
When they are all a part of my breed existing from the loins of me
I Pray even now for the seed I leave behind
Their struggles will be few and life for them will somehow be kind

I am ready to sleep
In a moment of eternal's peace
When I awake this time my pain will be alright
For in the arms of He who shines the light
I will rest
But before I do I must thank you My Dear
For making life it's Best
Don't you worry about me
I will wake up on the other side
In Pure Happiness

The Pain I Feel

My heart is sore pained with me:
and the terrors of death are fallen upon me.
Psalm 55:4

Oh My Lord I know you are here
Even in the midst of these fallen tears

Yet the pain I feel within
Causes me to doubt I will ever hear You again

I feel as if I will surely die
From the anguish that torments me inside

The emotions, the thoughts, the feelings in my soul
The aches, the grief has carved in me an empty hole

The pain I feel makes me so numb
I hide under my covers and regret the morning that will come

Others can't see the hurt I feel
So I must smile and grin
As I die within

How can one's Soul hurt so long and so deep
This pain that abides I feel even while I sleep

I hope as the days and nights come and fade
The grief the distress the heartache will all go away

The Pain I Feel

Though at this time my heart my mind my every emotion
Crashes against my Spirit like the wave collides a rock in the ocean

I do hear You My Lord in the distance of this hole in my soul
Thou in the midst of the thrashing
I wonder will I ever again be whole

My life before me has quickly diminished
With no joy no peace and no hope of love
My life to me may as well be finished

I lay and cry feeling as if I will surely die
I struggle to whisper silently a prayer from inside
That somehow, somehow Lord your hand will guide

I thank My Lord for the long awaited light
In the late night hour I heard Him cry
Hold on my child it will soon be alright
I got you day and night

He WILL Love you "through" and never let you go
The Father of All will hold you CLOSE in the midst of your pain
He will ROCK you like a Mother does her hurting child till the HURT
has GONE Away!!!

Thank You Daddy

The New Thing

*For they that are after the flesh
Do mind the things of the flesh;
But they that are after the Spirit
the things of the Spirit.
Romans 8:5*

I have been given a divine duty to do
I know I must continue until I am through
My time has divinely been occupied
From my one course time I must not allow to subside

Walking alone fixated on doing the Master's will
Excepting my destination with a heart of steel
Minding my own business so careful not to lean
I was taken notice to a New Thing

Now I find exquisitely I've been detained
Being pulled I do my best with what time remains
I must face the Will of God that I know is sure
Verses this New Thing that leads me to another course

I can't deny this New Thing is not a bore
But my steps I know are ordered by the Lord
My focus and time has now been split
But God's Will I don't want to quit

I hear a voice within
"Stand and do not bend
God is not a God who confuses or distract
There is only one path so repent
And get back on track"

I confess I am fascinated by this New Thing
Happiness and pleasures my *flesh* it brings
But I must surrender once again my all
And take heed to the Master's constant call

Perhaps this New Thing was not sent from above
But to distract me from my first Love
Yet I have desired this one thing
My God has promised to me He would bring

If I keep my focus on God above
Perhaps this New Thing
Can prove to be of the Master's Love

In God's time and truly not mine

"Give Me My Eagle's Wings"

(The righteous will fly)

*Though thou exalt thyself as the eagle,
and though thou set thy nest among the stars,
thence will I bring thee down, saith the Lord.*
Obadiah 4

Give me Lord my Eagle wings
Let me fly above my means
Why my Lord if I am A Eagle
Am I down here with these dead dried beetles

I look above my head
I see the birds that you Lord have fed
They fly high above this old ground
While I lift my head to hide a weary frown
The birds sit upon my fence singing songs of happiness
I know the songs that they sing
For it was I who taught them to praise the King
Here I am left to waddle with the chickens and the ducks
Lift me up Lord and rid me from this thing called bad luck

Give me Lord my Eagle's wings
So I can fly above my means
Why my Lord must life be so unfair
You told me you wouldn't put no more on me than I could bare
In that same day too
You told me you made me an Eagle
To speak for you
How can I speak to the Eagles
If I'm here on the ground with dead dried beetles

While kneeling down on my knees
I heard a soft faint scream
I looked up and all around
The voice seem to be coming from the ground
It was a beetle that wasn't dead at all
Get off me "help" he called
I stood very quickly and began to apology
He straighten his wings and flew up to the level of my eyes
No need to apologize
For it is you who bought me back alive
The beetle flew on his way
Flying higher and higher all that day
Then he sat on my fence
There with the birds singing songs of happiness

Give Me
My Eagle's Wings

Now I really cried in despair
Why my Lord is this life so unfair
Give me my Eagles wings
Let me fly above my means

Why must I be down here with the chickens and the ducks
They won't sing nor talk all they do is cluck
I am an Eagle and am down here on this ground
All day I lift my head to hide my weary frown

"Don't be so sad" I heard a voice say
"You are my hope of a brighter day"

I looked up and all around
Only to find the voice came from down on the ground
It was a duck that waddled so proud
He spoke again so clear and so loud

I know that you are an Eagle this is true
But I hope one day to be just like you
You are so "Righteous", you walk after the light
We know that you will always do what is right

Where, I ask did you learn to speak so grand
From you, he said I always hear you while you
Eat from the master's hand

While he yet spoke along came a chicken
He didn't cluck, no indeed
He sung in perfect harmony

Give Me
My Eagle's Wings

Where, I asked did you learn to sing so fine
From you, he said I hear you all the time singing
Praises in the sun shine
They waddled on down the road
Speaking and singing on one accord
I felt something good inside
What had happened at that time
I felt such a delight
I spread my wings and began to fly
I flew so high I could no longer see the birds
Sitting on my fence
Their joyful singing I wouldn't miss

I was an Eagle flying now where I belong
Up high with my own kind, here was my real home
Oh how good it felt to spread my Eagle wings
But suddenly I longed to be with the birds and hear them sing
Who will watch over them even the chickens and the ducks
If I'm not there they may forget how to sing
They won't talk they will only cluck

I tilted my wings and began to land
Now I can see the Master's plan
He needs me down on the ground
So His Love and Joy can be spread around
Being down here I am God's mouth, hands and feet
To guide others to a life that's complete
If I keep my Joy, don't complain, I can cope
So my Righteous Light will give others Hope
Now I know I can soar high at any time and return then again
To be the Master's Hand

I thanked the Lord for my Eagle Wings
He replied; "My son you had them all the time
The Joy of the Lord IS your Strength to fly"

"The Soul Of The Black Butterfly"

**Upon an instrument of ten strings,
And upon the psaltery; upon the harp
With a solemn sound. For thou, Lord,
Hast made me glad through thy work:
I will triumph in the works of thy hands.
Psalms 91:3-4**

Heartaches! Troubles! Sickness and Pain!
Trials! Tribulations, again and again!
Tossed about! Kicked around! Ridiculed . . .
And kicked to the ground
So many Tears! Too many Fears!
Yet she smiles, from ear to ear . . .

In spite of all she goes through
The Soul of the Black Butterfly
In anticipation, She soars to You.
Within Her Soul, She finds the Joy . . .
That she's so graciously been given to employ

Yes, the sound of the music down in Her Soul
Heals and sooths and makes Her whole
The rhythm of the drum, motivates Her to run

Mountains! Valleys! Deserts and Hills!
Rivers! Storms! Dark clouds She feels
Ostracized! Criticized! Mutilated! Accused!
Abused! "Deleted", after being Used
Yes, these are the forces that try to hold Her down
In spite of these life's oppositions
The Soul the Black Butterfly finds her culmination . . .
She rises and writes Her own composition

For the sound of the music down in Her Soul
Heals and sooths and makes Her whole
The Rhythm of the Drum
Motivates her to continue to run

All that I now encounter, I know is by Your Hand
Many have come to destroy Your plan
Yes, they try to divert my course
But the rhythm of the drum, beats with force

Within my Soul I feel the strength
Of the Butterfly Wings!!!
I feel the Rhythm that causes me to sing!!!
But now, Your Hand . . .

The Soul Of The Black Butterfly

Your Hand seems to have stopped me
It seems You have closed every door!
Though You have only caused me to become determined . . .
More determined Than ever before!

With my back against the wall . . .!
I'll stand! I'll stand still in the storm!
I'll walk through the valley tall!!
Yes I'll stand! I won't move!
I won't move off the wall!!!
No! I can't, I won't fall!

Within my Soul I feel the Butterfly Wings . . .!
The music that I hear tells me it's almost spring!!
At the drummer's beat!
I feel new movement in my feet!

But now what . . .!?
Why? Why must you be so cruel!?
You've bent me to my knees!
You've caused me to empty self, for You!
There's nothing left, within this shell . . .
That would hinder me, to rise and prevail!!

I feel the strength of the Butterfly Wings!
Down in my Soul new sounds now ring!
The thumping of the drum makes me to know
You will soon come . . .!

The Soul Of The Black Butterfly

But wait . . .!
Why!? Why now has the lights gone out!?
I can't see nor even feel my way about!
Troubles!? Troubles Lord!? We've had Troubles before . . .!
I called on you and you "made" a door!
I done well in time past
You taught me, Troubles come but they don't last

But these troubles, seem to be closing me in . . .
Even You Lord, seem to have left me, without a friend . . .

My Soul is weary, my Soul feels lost!
I struggle to find You, at any cost . . .!
The music is gone, the Drum has "stopped"!
The Soul of the Black Butterfly . . . drops!
"Perhaps " . . . I will die before I will ever fly . . .

There's no sound of music, in my soul
No music to Heal, to soothe nor to make me whole
Without the Drummer's beat
I feel such a defeat

It's the Rhythm of the Drum that motivates me to run
It's the sound of the music that keeps me singing
The beat of the drum that keeps the Joy bells ringing

The Soul Of The Black Butterfly

In the music I feel Your touch
It's the Rhythm of the Drum that I need, so much
Lord the beat of my heart, the breath I breathe . . .
Will all cease without Your hand to lead.
You, You are the music, I need . . .

I "now" see, I see the light, I see the stars and the moon!
All is brighter, troubles are lighter!!
I feel . . . I've been birth from a cocoon . . .

The sound of the music now returns!
To tell me there's "still" so much to learn
The Rhythm of the drum, floods my Soul
And from Your Hand . . .! The "real" me unfolds

The music from my Soul, has birth and made me whole!
My strength has been renewed, my hope renowned! I have new
vision!!
I've been tried and tested but my faith has been proved
It's taken time. Yes! It's taken pain! Many nights I had to cry
But the sound of the music kept me alive!!
By the beat of the Drum, I did survive!!!

With Power in my wings, I will fly to new sounds the music brings.
Yes, new challenges, New levels, new depths, new heights!
My butterfly wings will take me to never before flights!!

. . . .
. . . .

I thank God, for the sound of the music that will always be there
The Rhythm that I love, I will always keep near
Rather I fly, walk, crawl or run . . .
I will always move to the beat of One Drum.

I Am A Prisoner

For when ye were the servants to sin,
Ye were free from righteousness.
Romans 6:20

I am a prisoner of this world
Bounded till the day I die to sweat as I toil
Though I am free from the curse that binds the eternal soul
Free from the prince that holds earthly control

In this prison cell I walk unchained, complete and whole
Bounded only by moralistic righteousness
That has been given in my soul
I must stand up and walk in peace the peace
Yes, the peace that keeps me free

All around me is chaos that makes the weak do wrong
Though I am a prisoner to Right I must not rebel
For it is Right that makes me strong

Yes I am tempted on every side
The inmates sometimes they make me cry
I have real thoughts at times to break from this wicked cell
All those in this block are so treacherous they make my life pure hell

How did I get here in this locked cell???
What is my sentence?
What was my crime?
Who gave the verdict?
What is my time?

I was guilty at birth
Not fit to die
My soul of no worth
Innocence was my only alibi

I Am A Prisoner

The awaiting warden told many lies
He hoped the standing judgment against me
Would never subside

I had no money to offer yet I had nothing to conceal
Iwas given the highest paid Lawyer
That took my case to Calvary's Supreme Hill

Yes, I was found guilty
For a crime I could have never paid
My Lawyer stood all that l.o.n.g day
On my behalf with the Supreme judge He stood to say
Mercy Your Honor, Mercy
This debt I will pay

All charges were dropped and I was set free
To be a Prisoner of this world to help others to see
Until the day that I depart
I will keep the Key to this prison door in my heart
Down in my Righteous heart I too will cry
Mercy, Mercy Your Honor please
Set this one FREE

Distance Is My Child

For this my son was dead, and is alive again;
he was lost, and is found . . .
Luke 15:24

I gave birth to you and held you to my heart
Why is it now we are so far apart
From my tender breast you fed
It was I who helped you sound the very first word you said

I walked with you your first wobbling steps
As you ran and fell it was my out stretched hands you met
The nights you cried I held you in my loving arms
I kept you safe from your fears and unseen harm
When fever came my love and prayers
Cooled and comforted you from your stripped layers

It was I who taught you your charm to show
Your dazzling charisma from the world you are now told
Even with that I taught you to be kind
Think of others and never manipulate another's mind
Selfishness is not God's way
Giving and sharing will always put you ahead of the game
I led you on this path of righteousness
I Prayed night and day that you would always be safe and blessed

I have lived to this moment to see the results of my womb
A College degree/Military honors you should receive soon
You were the example for the next seed that would bloom
So all my offspring would walk in righteousness too

Distance Is My Child

Where are you now? Why have you gone astray?
So many nights I sit here and pray
My eyes are red and dim from the tears I now cry
But even now I pray for you an alibi

But in this meantime
Lord keep him, protect him
Help him to go the right way
Remind him daily that he must pray

So distance are you My Child
Yet the Lord loves you so much
How could you have ran so wild

My God yet promise I don't have to be afraid
From this bondage somehow you will be saved

"Regret"!!

Therefore remove sorrow from thy heart,
And put away evil from thy flesh: for
Childhood and youth are vanity
Ecclesiastes 11:10

Walking home the lingering reality
Of lost innocence found my hidden shame
I tried to fight the pretense of my mind
Had it really all started off as a simple game

Was this my hidden desire?!
For sure I was a woman now
A precious gift I was now without
Though I could not smile
No, I found nothing I could laugh about

This time nor place was not to be
I found myself losing to the tragedy of *blue*
The confusing sadness will now forever be
I know for sure the words he spoke were not true

If only I could go back
Standing at the door he would stay
For the price I have paid was much too high
The one thing I now lack
I now see I'll never get back
Only a night I wish I could forget
A moment in time I will always Regret

Too often young girls give up the most precious gift God has given. We, as women fail to honor Ourselves; by not standing in our integrity as Princess and the Queens God has made us. We must know we are His ordained Bride to be. Ladies you hold the POWER to save the young Prince and Kings from defiling their own virtuous temples before the Righteous Groom . . . Have "No Regrets"!! Just say NO—GO HOME!! There is no shame to WAIT for the Honey moon – The King of kings will be Pleased.

"The Heart Of A Prepared Bride"

And I John saw the holy City,
New Jerusalem, coming down
From God out of heaven, prepared
As a bride adorned for her husband.
Revelation 21:2

Make of me what You will
My whole self to you I yield

Unto you Lord I give
From here within where you want to live
This vessel made with your own hands
For you Master holds my divine plan

My Soul thirst for You
As a blade of grass for the morning dew
As I hunger at your feet
Feed me Lord till no more I can eat

Fill me now make me whole
My heart, my mind the depth of my soul
Saturate me with Your Glory
Let your Love and Peace unfold my story

Pour into me that which You want to pour out
Bring your Glory and Honor
From the fruits I will sprout

As a humble lamb that the shepherd must guide
Raise me Lord while in you I abide
And exalt me in Your due time
As your Spirit filled Prepared and Ready Bride

Are you a Prepared and Ready Bride?
Your heart must be stamp SOLD OUT before true righteous fruit will
sprout
The Groom waits for His Righteous Bride to have no doubts to Whom
they belong
Then and only then can we all go Home
Come on my Sister, my Brother yield all not just most
And let your heart be lead by the Holy Ghost
This is the heart of God's prepared Bride; She has already died
And now live only for the Master to Abide

Glitter N Gold

*If I have made gold my hope, or have said
to the fine gold, Thou art my confidence;
If I rejoiced because my wealth was great,
and because my hand had gotten much;
This also were an iniquity to be punished by the judge:
Job 31:24-25,28*

Glitter and Gold isn't what it's told
Fancy suits and diamond rings
Is less than what it seems
Prestige, respect, arrogant, intelligence
Is what's seen from the rich and proud
Though love and true happiness
Is what's missed from this crowd

Emerald green grass
Doesn't always last
The grass that seems greener on the other side
Has tics, Flees and other bugs that hide
Though unseen, draws the desire of one to be
Where beauty lies on surface but not beneath

Wash your face brush your teeth
Put on clean underwear and always dress neat
This will get you a good job so it's preached
But only what's on the inside
Will enable you so your job you will keep

The company you keep tells a lot about you
Perhaps at times this is true
So a bum, an addict and a thief
Can dress and walk with a Priest
Now who's the bum, addict and who's the thief
Perhaps the Priest!?

Mmmmm . . .?

Glitter and Gold isn't always
What it's told

Vanity, Vanity all is but Vanity
Once *you* unfold . . .

Be Here Now

But godliness with contentment is great gain.
For we brought nothing into this world, and it
Is certain that we can carry nothing out.
1 Timothy 6:6-7

Today is the beginning of the rest of your life
The one who died has already paid the price
So you and I can live eternal life
Now take your time and get it right

There really is no need to hurry no need to fret
Not one Soul has taken control of their life by worry yet

That which you desire will come
Worry will only cause you to miss
Where and from whom "it" has come from

So be here now, now is where you are
Don't look back nor compare
Where another have come or how life's unfair

Don't you worry what you may lack
God's got your back and will carry you far
All in time you will be that appointed star

Remember to breathe in slow relax and let time flow
Take it slow don't move too fast
Savor the moment for the moment won't last

One thing I have learned
You must be where you are now–or-
You will miss what is for you to learn
If you are here while somewhere else you yearn

So be here now, now is where you are
You must be true to yourself
Before you can be true to someone else–
This would even hinder you from being true to the Master's Rule

"Eyes Of Vision"

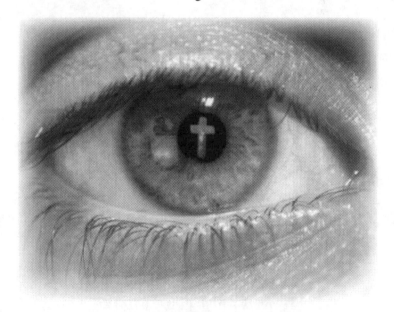

We walk by faith, NOT by sight:
2 Corinthians 5:7

No matter what life bring your way
No matter what others may say
By your faith you can see
In your Vision what will be

They say the eyes are the window to the soul
So close your eyes and Vision yourself whole

You have been told the door is closed
Another holds the key
But in your eyes you can see a brand new door
That will set you free

No matter what life brings your way
No matter what others may say
The Vision lies within your eyes

Set your sight on your goal
Close your eyes and search you soul

In your sight there is a wall
But in your Vision it is resolved

No matter what life brings your way
No matter what others may say
By your faith you can see
In your vision what will be

There's a mountain standing tall
It's so big and you're so small
Where's your faith
A grain of mustard seed is all it takes

Eyes Of Vision

Close your eyes
With Eagle wings you can fly
You can soar high over that mountain
Where your destiny lies

No matter what life may bring your way
No matter what others may say
The answer lies within your eyes

Someone may say "No-stop-you can't"
But those negative seeds you don't have to plant

Close your eyes and visualize
The path in which have been set
And day by day you will see
That which is perfect

No matter what life may bring your way
No matter what others may say
By your faith you can see
In your Vision what will be

Please remember it is true
The "Vision" has been planted
But not by you

The question is asked
Is it according to your faith
How long the "Vision" will take

No matter what life brings your way
No matter what others may say
The Vision lies within your eyes

Eyes Of Vision

The Vision has been given to you
With set orders what to do
The Master is trusting in you
To see the "Vision" through

Are you waiting on The "Vision"
Or is the vision waiting on you

No matter what life may bring your way
No matter what others may say
By your faith you can see
In your Vision what will be

Are you standing / moving/ waiting in faith
Or have you lost the battle it takes?
The "Vision" comes forth only with courage
Dig down deep you have so much in storage

By Faith you can stand strong
If you take too long the Master will move on

For the "Vision" is neither yours nor mine
Someone ready is next in line

The "Vision" is *set* for an appointed time
It shall come forth and not lie

God's Will will be done
By you or another chosen One

The Hands Of The Black Man

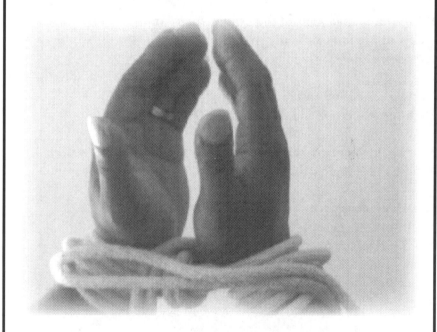

I will therefore that men pray everywhere,
Lifting up holy hands, without wrath and doubting.
1 Timothy 2:8

Where are the hands of the black Man
Once picking cotton in the fields
From his land of riches
His freedom they did steal

His hands were strong his heart was proud
His soul was bound yet his God he found

Where were the hands of the proud black Man
Cuddled around his family so tight
Afraid the Massa would take them by night

Not too proud to bend his knees
He lifted his hands and cried please God deliver me

Where oh where are the hands of the black Man
Where is the hand of a real black Man

Not all was enslaved; being black many pave the way
Benjamin Banneker a scientist
Martin Delaney a physician said to be the best
Henry Blair an inventor of a corn harvest plow
These three were among the first of many
To show the black Man how

Benjamin T. Montgomery indeed a Man of color
Set in his mind to invent a boat propeller
Thou he never became a free Man in his time
That did not stop the inventions in his mind

The Hands Of The Black Man

He like many others invented to make the work easier and faster
But their ideals were taken by their own slave masters

These were the hands of Real black Men
Who had to steal away just to pray
While another sinned with their mate
They stood together and help each other with a grin
In the midst of it all they trusted God to the end

"To the back of the bus Rosa Parks"
Why? She exclaimed, because my skin is dark
Martin Luther King had a dream
Are we living today what he seen?

Many years have come and past
The black man's hands were free at last
Free to do as he pleased
So it was said but was it true indeed
Where oh where are the hands of the black Man
Where is the hand of a proud black Man
Free to do as he can?
Free from the hand of another Man?
Free to make his own life plans?
Mmmm?
Now here are the hands of a Free Black Man
True, no longer does he have to run and hide
Just to lift his hands to the sky
But look at the hands of a Free Black Man

While it is true no longer he has to pray
His family they don't take away
Why can't it be seen
His family is being stolen by deeper means?

Now here are the hands of a Free Black Man
His hands, He has chosen to bind again
No not with chains nor a whip
Bound again the black Man has been tricked

Taken from the Mother Land was not so bad
Now killing his own is much MORE sad
Where are the hands of the FREE black Man?

Passing guns and dealing drugs not even far from home
Now he has become an enemy of his own
Tricked by the hands of the one who's kept him down too long

Wake up Black Man and look around
Don't be caught with your pants hanging down
Take the Hand of another not the life of others
Help your Brother from another Mother
Respect your Sister by another Mister

Where are the hands of God's black Man!?
Where are the hands of a Righteous Man?
His hands are strong and full of power
Yet he rejects the God who delivered him in his darkest hour

God's black man thinks it makes him weak
To be found among the righteous and the meek
While some how he thinks macho arrogance makes him strong
Is it because he's been put down far too long

Where are the hands of a Successful Black Man
Far from Home he lies in the arms of a foreign land
While his own Community cries for an influential Black Hand
Wake up black Man and look around

So many are becoming brown
Should we smile or should we frown
Could it be another way to separate and destroy our ground
Or is it God's way of turning what was
made wrong back around . . .?
Bringing back the first from many births

Where are the Hands of the intelligent Black Man?
Oppressed, Depressed, brought down low
He wonders where did Daddy go
Now with welfare hand-outs
The dream of college is a doubt

Another trick of the enemy
To take the black man's drive
And leave him hopeless
With a false since of pride

The question has been ask where are all the black Men at
The answer came back in reply
Behind bars or in the grave they lie
Is this where the hands of the black Men hide

Open your eyes Black Man while you can
He who dictates is not your friend
He is out to stop the Black Man's Hand

Where are the Hands of a Wise Black Man?

With all of life's disasters
Now is not the time to run from the Holy Master
For the one in this land, strives to confuse your Hand
He seeks to weaken your numbers and catch you in a slumber
So he'll hold the power to destroy you in this last hour

The Hands Of The Black Man

Don't you know Black Man, you are known to be
The strongest, most powerful, dominating seed
God has given you in your genes
What other men only hope and dream

Yes, we all know that it's true
Medically, Scientifically and Spiritually proven
You are the most perfect specimen of all God's humans

Throughout the ages of time
God has strengthen the Black Man's Hand
The enemy has tried time and again to KILL his Spirit within
But it won't be done for the Hands of the Black Man
Has already WON
God has eternally provided the Plan
All he has to do is hold to the Master's Hand

So where are the Hands of today's FAITHFUL Black Man?
Yes, he Stands in VICTORY by God's Conquering
Hand of POWER . . .!
Go ahead raise your Hands and Praise Him Black Man
It Is Your Divine HOUR

Step For Step

Order my steps in thy word:
And let not any iniquity have
Dominion over me
Psalm 119:133

I can make it I can do this
I must remember to be consistent with time
step for step I can master this quest

One day at a time
Minute for minute
There is no hurry for time is not mine
I'll be here tomorrow
To climb another step
I will not stress my self
I'll only do my best
Step for step

I mustn't try to do it all in one day
Rome wasn't built that way
And still today it stands
Because they followed the Divine plan
Step for step

When it all seems too overwhelming
I'll stand back and take a breath
Count to ten and then take a rest
I'll remember He'll never give me too much
Without a mighty touch

I know each step makes me more prepared
So I can journey on my quest
With unassuming confidence
Step for step

If I am faced with this test
It is only because He knows I'll conquer it
Step For Step
And be ready for my next waiting quest
Step For Step

Do You Know How The Story Goes?

How art thou fallen from heaven,
O Lucifer, son of the morning! How art thou cut down
To the ground, which didst weaken the nations! . . .
I will ascend above the heights of the Clouds,
I will be like the most High.
Yet thou shalt be brought down to hell,
to the sides of the pit.
Isaiah 14:12, 14-15

If you don't know how the story goes
I'm here to tell you so you'll know

Jesus came to fight the battle
So you and I won't have that hassle

The battle began at heaven's door
With God and His most beautiful angel, Lucifer

> If you don't know how the story goes
> I'm here to tell you so you'll know

Lucifer wanted more power than God had gave
Already higher than all other angels, he was made

God proclaimed I am Alpha and Omega
The Beginning and the End
If you stay you will obey
Or you will become my enemy and not my friend

> If you don't know how the story goes
> I'm here to tell you so you'll know

Do You Know How The Story Goes?

Michael an archangel was called to God's side
The message he was given was, tell Lucifer good-bye

Lucifer roared and raged that day
Then out he went through heaven's gate

If you don't know how the story goes
I'm here to tell you so you'll know

Lucifer or Satan he's now called
Turned his anger from God to us all

No match was he for God Almighty
So in the earth he strives to destroy God's army
He battles with you and me so we'll lose hope of eternity
With God the Father King of kings
But Victory has already been won through Jesus Christ the Son

That's how the story went ... Now you know why JESUS was sent!

The thief cometh not, but for to steal, and to kill, and to destroy:
I am come that they might have life, and that they might have
It more abundantly. St. John 10:10

"Don't Bury Me Wounded"

A certain man went down from Jerusalem to Jericho,
And fell among thieves,
which stripped him of his raiment,
And wounded him, and departed,
leaving him half dead.
Luke 10:30

journeyed in darkness descending from my climb
I come to you for a bit of your time
The burses and wounds I've gathered along the way
Have caused me great intense pain
From my exterior I may not look like much
But my soul needs a loving aiding touch
All I ask is for a chance
Please don't judge me at a glance

Don't Bury Me Wounded
Don't push me away
Because my yesterday was not as your today

You told me what I already knew
How Jesus cared and died for All not just a few
Though I reached out for your love
You told me about the One above
I needed to talk to a listening ear
You told me how I am not to fear
Just an embrace of tender care
Somehow that was a gesture unfair

Don't Bury Me Wounded
Don't push me away
Because my yesterday was not as your today

Within this injured shall
I am a whole person as well
A person that's been through lasting hell
I come to you in desperate need
Holding on to the very breath I breathe
I need your helping hand
Not just a "God bless you-Amen"!
I have been hurt and wounded from the inside out
Please don't just pray for me
While at the meal table my name is tossed about

Don't Bury Me Wounded
Don't push me away
Because my yesterday was not as your today

"Don't Bury Me Wounded" (Cont...)

I came to you with a broken heart
My soul torn in many parts
In a state of mind totally lost and confused
I needed to know how I was to be used
You taught me but only in part
You failed to walk in God's Love and stay within the Ark

Don't Bury Me Wounded
Don't push me away
Because my yesterday is not as your today

If with no more than just a feather
We are all in this boat together
Trying to make it to the other side
Many gifts God gave
But only one Spirit to lead this Holy way

It is confirmed that Jesus to all He feeds
Yet if Jesus was all we need
On the earth seated He would be
We are all here one for another
Not predicated upon mother, father, sister or brother
Although He is God Almighty
The plan is for you and I to stand united

Don't Bury Me Wounded

So don't you Bury Me Wounded
Don't push me Away
Because my yesterday was not as your today

While I fade within from my open wounds
You choose to ignore me as if I was hidden in a cocoon
A band-aid on an open wound that needs to be sealed
Will never allow the deepness of the cut to heal

Please Don't Bury Me Wounded
Please don't push me away
I was sent to you for your aide
So My Tomorrow won't be as My Today

Please, Please!
"DON'T BURY GOD'S PEOPLE WOUNDED"
God has called you to be His
Hands-Feet-and His Mouth
WWJD
do it!
In Jesus Name

Evil Is Present

Then when lust hath conceived,
It bringeth forth sin: and sin, when
It is finished, bringeth forth death.
James 1:15

What do you do when everything in you wants to do wrong
How do you fight temptation that won't let you stand strong

When you know you are already weak
Into sinful diversions you want desperately to creep

Oh–no, you can't tell a lie
Your thoughts and feelings you don't want to hide

If it were possible to enjoy the sins of desire
The thoughts of the flesh, for just one night
And return back untarnished to paradise
Yes Lord I admit
For just one night You I would quit

But I know it is impossible for he who is clean
To hide among sin and not be seen

Why is it Lord my old ways I fight
You told me I am new since I found the light

The law I live by is God's righteousness
But in my flesh I see there is no holiness

Must I struggle with doing that which is right
Lord will you still love me when I stand in you sight

Help me Lord to win this battle we must fight

"Come to the Lord on your knees
"With persistence you can resist the devil
And he WILL flee"

"I Met An Angel Today"

Be not forgetful to entertain strangers:
for thereby some have entertained angels
unawares.
Hebrews 13: 2

I Know I met an angel today
An elderly lady passed my way
Her hands were full as she approached the door
As she reached for the knob her favorite scarf she dropped

She bent down at her waist
And her weekly items from her bag escaped
Reaching to save what she hoped to store
She was bumped from behind and knocked to the floor
People passed briskly by
As if not to even see her nigh

As she arose to her feet
A pair of shoes she heard squeak
Stepping on her favorite scarf
Nearly broke her peaceful heart

As she pulled it from the ground
Another bumped her spinning her around
Catching her balance she reached for her bag
Bumped again some one said "excuse me, move, you old hag"

Down she went and there she sat
She shook her head looked around
To see where all her items were at

She couldn't believe not a single soul stopped to give her a hand
She watched them move in their own directions
Walking as quickly as any one can

She reached first for her purse
Observing her shopping bag being dispersed
While she secured her purse between her teeth
Her .89 cent can of tuna rolled from her reach

She struggled desperately to her feet
While gathering all she could reach
Placing the items in her bag she was again
Knocked to her knees

She dropped her bag from her hands
And watched her items roll again
She reached again for that scarf
And at that moment it was kicked to far

She sat in the mist of all those busy feet
With her purse still between her teeth
She paused placing her purse between her legs
Knowing all she could do was sit and pray

A feeling of sadness covered her heart
What has happened to the people to make
Righteousness so far from their heart
No kindness, no patience, no time to care
Such a selfish, hopeless spirit in the air

I won't be defeated I heard her say
As she rose to her feet non-afraid
She looked for her shopping bag that was just in sight
She then turned around and was blinded by a light

A stranger stood right before her
with her shopping bag now full and her purse
She touched his hand, smiled then said
Thank You Sir,
For a moment I thought I've been cursed

He smiled back as he opened the door
don't be discourage He said your prayer has been heard

I'm not discourage she eagerly said, I know there's yet hope for all
And don't you stop praying so you won't be lost; she added
He nodded then said; oh, Ma'am your scarf

I Met An Angel Today

With her shopping bag, her purse and now her favorite scarf
She smiled and looked up
Then patted my little head and filled My emptied cup

I turned with excitement to see the old lady one last time
I really wanted to say good-bye
I wanted to tell her how I admired her tenacity
How she continued to be kind she didn't sit and cry

How she exhibited such a Godly Spirit of no fear
But just like that, like magic she had disappeared

Beside me was her shopping bag and purse nice and neat
All of a sudden my stiff cripple feet was dangling with relief

I stood from that chair and shouted an open prayer
Thank You Jesus!! and please except a hug
From the Angel you sent to help me stand up!!!
As I dropped my head from the sky
That favorite scarf fell
And I heard a soft voice say this is NOT Good-bye

"Build A Fence Around Me"

He that dwelleth in the secret place of the
Most High shall abide under the shadow
Of the Almighty.
Psalm 91:1

Lord Build a fence around me
Keep the enemy off my path
While you direct my steps to Righteousness

I Long for Your arms of Love to shield around me
To comfort, protect and even to hide me
Keep me from the hand of my enemy
Who searches desperately to find me

Keep me Lord in the shadow of Your wings
For even in Your shadow I am safe from the troubles
The adversary brings.

Build a Fence all around me My Precious Lord
Keep the devil off my path
As You direct my steps to Righteousness

I Praise Your Hand that makes and mold
That loves and guides and has control
I look to You to cover me
From the one who seeks to hinder thee

Meet me Lord in that secret place
There I long to enter from the long day's chase
Here in Prayer I am covered by Your Divine Grace
As I Pray

Build A Fence All around me
Keep the devil off my path
As You direct my steps in Righteousness

Keep me from the one who tries constantly to devour me
Who comes to detour me from my destiny
If you Lord order my daily steps
Then in safety I will be kept

With Your hedge all about me
I know I am safe and I am set free
From the treacherous weapon of the enemy

Thank you Lord for Your ANGELS
That Encamps as a Fence all about me

"Clean In Side Out"

And the Lord said unto him,
now do ye Pharisees Make clean the outside of the cup
and the platter;
But your inward part is full of ravening and
wickedness.
Luke 11:39

I stand here beneath the water's fall
It cleans my body outside
Yet am I clean in all

My mind, my heart the water don't touch
It is here where can't be seen
Where cleansing is needed so much
So how does one cleanse the heart and mind
From the ways and thoughts
That destroys and binds?

Baptism I've heard does indeed save
But the filth of the flesh
It won't fade

I must strive to be clean inside
Trusting Him that awaits
To purify

The word of God is what I need
In the beginning the Word I read
Was made flesh so I can see

So if Jesus is the Word, it is He that I must follow
He will lead me to that cleansing water
Then fill this vessel that is empty and hollow

The more I read the more I learn
For my sinful ways, Lord I don't want to burn

Jesus died to make me whole
He shed his blood to cleanse my soul

Clean In Side Out

Now I accept the Lord in my heart
By His Holy Spirit I will go far

My Gifts have come without repentance
But now Your anointing grips my soul
With lasting Clinches

Here I am before You Lord
To sanctify this Vessel to its core

With more of you my Lord please fill
Fill me Lord and let it spill
Yes, fill and let it over flow
To this outside shell let You show

Run, Daddy run down until your Divine Glory glows
With more fruit that spurts
From the Inside–Out
Run, Daddy run from the Inside–Out

With His Righteousness you will conquer this new birth
And never return to the prince of this earth

I believe and I do not doubt–
Jesus died so 'we' can be forever Clean *Inside Out*

"Everyone Is Searching"

*And the word was made flesh, and dwelt among us,
(And we beheld his glory, the glory as of the only
Begotten of the Father,) full of grace and truth.
St. John 1:14*

hy are so many searching for what has already been told
Christ came from Glory to earth so the truth would unfold
Why then are so many living in sadness with their heads hung down
They feel as if there is no hope and for hell they are still bound

Many search for love, happiness and lost dreams
They feel no hope, nor direction for their destiny
They search for God and answers to all truth
Yet they fail to hear what's been given with all proof

The truth is not lost nor is it far
He is standing at the door knocking at every man's heart
Man has been searching since the beginning of time
Trying to reach a god they still can't find

Jehovah God Almighty loves us so much
That he sent his Son to end the search of such
Jesus, the Son of the Living God stood before us all
He walked the earth in God's Glory
Everyman He now calls

So why are so many still searching for what has already been told
Christ came from Glory to earth so the truth would unfold

Everyone Is Searching

Many has come to understand that man is a tri-unity
He is spirit with a soul yet the body only is seen
So the search is on to feed all three
Intensely man strives to feel that "he" is free

Gyms, spas, souped-up-hotrods
Scientology, Yoga, Buddhism and even Astrology
Money, music, sex, wine & dinning, entertainment at its best
Yes, he'll even go to the extreme with dangerous activities
Hand gliding, bungee-jumping, skate boarding on a ledge
So much excitement living on the edge

Man tries so hard to find what's missing inside
Trying to fulfill that where only God can abide
Searching still for joy, peace, yes real happiness
Forgetting God's demand for true righteousness

He struggles to find
The answer to the questions that boggles his mind
Answers that would help him to cope
Without, he feels lost with no hope

"Everyone Is Searching" (Cont....)

Only a fool searches for something that has already been found
Running from the truth he keeps his own soul bound
Only a darkened mind would risk his life for a moment's pleasure
Allowing his flesh to dictate rather earthly or heavenly treasures

Don't "judge" we all were blinded fools before we seen the light
Thank God we now know Jesus the Christ
Who died and made the ultimate sacrifice
So now you can be thankful you found the truth
Yes, Jesus died for me and for you

You look up at the cross
There you find many hung and were still lost

But your search is over only if you understand
It was the blood of Jesus the Christ and not that of just a man
The blood that Jesus shade on Calvary's Hill
Gives us strength & power and by His Spirit we are filled
If we only believe, from this world we are sealed

But it did not end on the cross or we all would still be lost
The victory came from the grave
Because He got up on that third and mighty day
This is why we ALL can today be saved

Everyone Is Searching

From hell back to Glory
He sits now and waits for you to tell His Story

So why are so many yet searching and empty at their end
Perhaps they need to be told the meaning of Easter is only where it began
Yes, so God and man can again be friends
Remember; Jesus left His Spirit and gave us Power
To tell ALL men who searches in their darkest hour

He died and rose again but that is not where The Story ends

Who are you telling; "He's an L-o-n-g Life FRIEND"
If you share with just one; "Jesus lives"
That one will tell one and soon it would be ten
The Search would be over for one more lost pondering soul!
All because ONE 'His Story' you told!

Yesterday's Struggles

And the Lord shall make thee the head,
And not the tail;
And thou shalt be above only,
And thou shalt not be beneath;
If that thou hearken unto the
commandments of the Lord,
Thy God which I command thee this day,
To observe and to do them:
Deuteronomy 28:13

How did I rise so high
When did yesterday's struggles pass me by

I did not realize how far I had come
I failed to see just what you Lord had done

In the midst of climbing I focused my eyes
I spoke only of my soon to be prize

I refused to look back, down or around
Especially when it seemed as if my feet
Were stuck in the ground

A many of days I journeyed alone
Friends had come and soon were gone
Even now I look around and don't see many
But as long as I have you Lord I have plenty

It was my Praises in my lowest days
That kept me from falling away

For many days I've Prayed and yes I cried
Lord please elevate me on high
Keep me humble at your feet
Give me Power so my enemy I will defeat

For so long I walked the dry desert ground
Now at last the flowing fountain I have found
Truly it is the Anointing that has made the difference

I still feel the old thrust from the valley low
Even while the Mighty Wind of the Mountain blows

Finally I have more to give than just that within
I can pull others from where I've been
I lift my hands up to the sky
I shout to the One who has lifted me on high

Somehow I always knew that one day I would succeed
Now yesterday's struggles are today's Victory
And as I breathe on tomorrow
I will yet Praise him for His Glory-Majesty and Power

He Leadeth Me

Then was Jesus led up of the
Spirit into the wilderness to be
Tempted of the devil.
Matthew 4:1

He leads me
In pastures green?
Not always . . .
Sometimes He Who Leads,
Doesn't seem to know best
He who leads in kindness leads me
In what seems to be a mess
The sun don't always shine down between the trees
Instead He leads where heavy shadows be
Toady the sun shines warm, soft and bright
Tomorrow's sunshine leads into the darkest night,
So whether in the green or desert land
I trust although I may not understand.

He Leads me
By still waters?
No, not always so . . .
Sometimes He who Leads
Surrounds me with heavy tempests that blow
My eyes sometimes flood with water that fills my soul
Nevertheless, when the storms beat hard and no more I can cry
In the night I know, the Master stands by
He whispers to my soul
"Lo, it is I
Above the tempest storm I hear your cry
Beyond this darkness is a table I have prepared
Alone this path I lead to show you I care"

He Leadeth Me

So whether on the mountain high
Or it be sunless valleys nigh
Even shadows of death may lie
But He is my Shepherd
And I need not cry for I am not alone
So I will not fear as He leads me home
Now where He leads, I can safely go
And not many days after, I shall surely know
Why in His wisdom, He has led me so
I only need to remember, He is my Shepherd
This if I never doubt
I am for certain I'll never be without

For the Lord Is My Shepherd
And that I know
I shall not want wherever I may go . . .

Defeatism And Criticism

And the tongue is a fire, a world of iniquity:
So is the tongue among our members, that it
Defiles the whole body, and sets on fire the course of
nature; and it is set on fire of hell.
James 3:6

I have given my whole life to my children's raising
I've never had the time to deal with my own up-bringing
I still have wounds that I have placed band-aids on
These wounds remind me how I too have been torn
I have tried not to become disgusted
With all of life's dreams being busted

I wrestle with "defeat" in my head
Because of "words" that have been said
Whoever said "words don't hurt"
Switches, sticks and stones
They tried to break my bones
But their words are like dirt
They stick down in the crevices of your mind
And gnaw at your very soul for all of time

"Life and death" are in the power of *one* tongue
It can free or bind anyone
Pain oozes from yet open wounds
Like *words* that play back from a song ending too soon

I must move past the "Critics" somehow
For I am so far behind the desires of the One to whom I bow
For sure someone without the wounds I bare
Could step into my life and make it "fly" like wings on air
I know My Father, has not dealt me a bad hand
I just never know what card to play or when to stand
This perplexity in my head keeps me in such doubt
Not having one to lead
Keeps me in contempt and tossed about

A hand full of cards
For a game that seems too hard
Pulled from a single deck
I am left only to expect . . . They all can't be bad
Though this hand has only made me sad
Even when I study long
The card I pick still
Winds up being wrong

Or it's always just a little too late

Defeatism And Criticism

Too many mistakes to ever make straight
Too late to pray for His loving Grace

Defeatism and Criticism plaques my soul
My open wounds claim control
How can I win . . .
With a hole that constantly pulls me in

I Pray every day to acquire the King of all Hearts
That's the One–Wild "Card" that can give me a clean start
For the hand He holds has slaughtered Defeatism
While His deck annihilate the one who bought Criticism
His hand will change my despair into Joy
His hand will deal me Peace so I'm not annoyed

The joker is "Wild"!
For those that sit among the wrong crowd
But The King of Kings beats the joker of this world hands down
Loose from the Cross by His Spirit I'm no longer lost
No longer do I have to cover my wounds
The words of the past can't boast like a tycoon

Defeatism and Criticism must move aside
For now I have a new life

I am told if I am bold
I can do all things through Jesus the Christ
For in the midst of the battle He has WON My SOUL

A Seed To Grow

Either make the tree good and his fruit good;
or else make the tree corrupt, and his fruit corrupt:
for the tree is known by his fruit. Matthew 12:33

Have I sown a seed In your life
Have I planted a tree
That will produce a paradise

We Have been sat upon a particular path
We never know how long it will last

We may journey together only for a little while
Together we strive to grow in wisdom
And keep a pleasant smile

Quickly you have come
And much to soon you must journey on

Have I sown a seed in your life
Have I planted a tree of paradise

Have I helped you along your way
Have I given you a brighter day

Everyone we meet on our course
Has been provided as a source

Have my words caused you to know
Something that will help you to grow

Will you be able to plant a seed
That will grow and fulfill another's need

Is there a ripe fruit upon your tree
Is it sweeter or is it bitter because of me

Can you now journey alone
Knowing to whom you will always belong

Have the power of Prayer been cultivated
While the presence of God has become uncomplicated

Have I received
What you have been given for me???

Don't be deceived every good Gift begins with
Serving and Giving of God's currency
Your Tithes and Offering are your best sown Seed

Plant A Seed Today . . .

A Time Of Silence

HOW LONG WILT THOU FORGET ME,
O LORD? FOR EVER?
HOW LONG WILT THOU HIDE THY FACE FROM
ME?
Psalm 13:1

I lie upon my bed in silence
Silence, silence within, silence all about
Silence all around me
There seems to be silence beyond a doubt

I wonder is this the end for me
Is my destination now complete?
Have I accomplished that which I was sent to meet?
Why is He so silent from me?

I look about as I look within and all is still
My joy, my hope, my daily drive I cannot feel
The voice that calls me to stand
To give thanks, to worship and to praise
Has all slipped away like sand
Though my busy, weary hands I raise

As Job I go forward and backward but cannot see Him
I feel as though I'm looking through a darken film
I look on the left to see His working hand
But there is no vision or mighty plan
I look on the right and He is hidden from my sight

When God is silent with you
Honestly, you want to renege
And be silent too

I know I must keep my life's promise
"In all things I'll give thanks"
Though from my daily worship
As I struggle to commune I draw a blank

A Time Of Silence

Absent of a touch from His anointed hand
You long for the dew of the Spirit once again
But all is still from the once constant spin
Nothing moves from the well within

As Job I ask this question too
Why is all so Silent – What did I do!?
Why from heaven nothing leaks…?
Then in a still soft voice the Lord finally speaks

"I know the way you take
Your foot has held My steps
My way you have kept
My words you continued to speak bold
You too shall come forth as gold
Just as my servant Job"

So please, please when you are in
A Time of Silence
Be faithful and stay confident
The Master is pleased with your vivaciousness
Never let your hunger quit
The water for your thirst He is sending
Hold on
He's unfolding your latter ending
He's preparing it greater than your beginning
You ARE a Blueprint to His Master Plan
You are still in His Mighty hand

Shhh… don't worry and don't you cry
Read the book of Job you will see why…

And on the seventh day God ended his work which he had made;
and he rested on the seventh day from all his work which he had made.
Genesis 2:2

…and all was silent, silence was everywhere

Do You Know Him By Name

Neither is there salvation in any other:
For there is none other Name under
Heaven given among men, whereby
We must be saved.
Acts 4:12

Do you know my God by name?
The ONE and ONLY True LIVING God!
Do you know Him in his Glory?
Have you met Him through His divine story?
Is He so real to you that you know He's with you all the time?
Do you laugh and talk during your intimate dine
Does He show you things to come and even things you've done?
Things that wasn't so pleasing to His Son
Does His presence make you cry?
Does He so tenderly dry your eyes?
Have you promised to walk upright and never to stray
Do you wake up giving God the Glory each day
Do you have a special time and place to pray
Yes, this is how we conquer our daily fight
Through Prayer he makes everything right
Yes, He forgives you when you've done wrong
Once you have repented, you will once again be strong
Has He given you his Heavenly tongues?
Have you taken time to praise Him for today's battle won?
Yes, He's drawing you to your knees
Open your mouth and let Him speak
He wants to water the Heavens and establish your seed
He sees and feels what you breathe
Do you believe he can even hear you when you sneeze?
He's not a God only in your mind; He has been here throughout time
He is not a God without a face and only one name
The God I know has a Glorious face and many Names
For He is a God that states many claims
When you look in the mirror I declare God is there
Your hands, feet and mouth He has to use
Yes, your frail body He wants to choose
No not to spread "religion" but to live within
So you and He can build relationship and become best of friends
How powerful is that thought?
To be called a friend of the mighty one
Who won the greatest battle ever fought
Powerful, Yes Power is his game and one of His many names
Do you need a Miracle? Well don't get cynical

With faith, a true optimistic and never a pessimist
You can have anything on your desired list
Learn to call Him by Name and you'll be surprised
How fast you can possess your claim
When you call on His many Names Power it brings
From the heavens into the earth where miracles are birthed

Here below are only a few of His powerful names to know
Don't be dismayed, there are more than this one book
can possibly hold
Yes, this is just a glimpse of God's many Names

EL SHADDAI–All-Sufficient One
JEHOVAH–Unchangeable, Intimate God
JEHOVAH ELOHEENU–The Lord Our God
JEHOVAH M'KADDESH–The Lord My Sanctifier
JEHOVAH SHALOM–My Peace and Wholeness
ELOHIM–God Our Sovereign, Mighty Creator
JEHOVAH ELOHAY–The Lord My God
JEHOVAH MAKKEH–The Lord Who Molds Me
JEHOVAH NISSI-The Lord My Banner of Victory
EL-ELOHE-ISRAEL–The Personal God of Israel
JEHOVAH ROHI–The Lord My Shepherd
JEHOVAH ROPHE–The Lord that Heals Me
JEHOVAH JIREH–The Lord My Provider
ADONAI–Lord and Master
JEHOVAH GMOLAH–The Lord Who Rewards
JEHOVAH SHAMMAH–God IS There
EL ELYON–God Most High
JEHOVAH TSABAOTH–The Lord of Hosts
JEHOVAH TSIDKENU–The Lord My Righteousness

Now you know his many Names but the one most powerful name
today will be the same tomorrow as yesterday and forevermore . . .
JESUS: is that Name the ONE, the ONLY True and LIVING GOD
JESUS: the Name the whole World will know
JESUS: the Name that causes demons to flee and evil must go

Do You Know Him By Name

JESUS: the Name Heaven bows to with glorious praises
JESUS: the Name that causes Hell to tremble even today
JESUS: is the name that every tongue one day will confess
Is LORD
and every knee will bow down to
Yes, even the so call atheist will have to say
JESUS IS LORD;
He is King of kings, the Lion of Judah
the Lily of the valley, the bright and morning star,
JESUS is the way out of no way,
He is the wheel in the middle of the wheel
THE SAVIOUR OF THE WORLD-OF EVERY LOST SOUL
For He is THE GREAT I AM
and He promises to be the "I AM"
Whenever
Whatever
Wherever you need Him to be

AMEN / AMEN

"Within My Mind"

Let this mind be in you,
Which was also in Christ Jesus:
Philippians 2:5

I live within my mind
The mind of Christ
Who truly Sacrificed
For all my idle time

A mind of hopes and dreams
A mind of which fantasies brings
Only possibilities

I live within my mind
The mind of Christ
Who truly Sacrificed
For all my idle time

Outside my mind there are doubts and fears
With hopelessness
Outside my mind there are dark cloudy days
With nights that seem endless
Outside my mind I have no direction to go
My path is dim and my course is much too slow

I live within my mind
The mind of Christ
Who truly Sacrificed
For all my idle time

Within My Mind

In my mind I stand on hopes there are no room for doubts
In my mind I know by faith I can push every dream out
In my mind I don't just fantasy I confess
It is a reality that has yet to manifest . . .

An idle mind really is the devil's workshop
So go ahead dream, dream big, don't stop
If you dare to decree and declare
What you speak will be released in the air
SO be sure your thoughts are Purified
So only God is Glorified

Dare to reach for that dream inside your mind
If it is of Christ
What He provides will Suffice
As long as you pushed through idle time
Within your mind.

Remember it is true only what you do for Christ will last
So look up, stretch towards your future and let go of your past

The Promise I Dream

For the vision is yet for an appointed time,
but at the end It shall speak, and not lie:
Though it tarry, wait for it; because it will
surely come, it will not tarry.
Habakkuk 2:3

Day Dreaming, perhaps it may seem
When my eyes are closed as well as open
I see my every promise as in a dream

I await to live that which I feel so deep
and dream even in my sleep
I wonder why I was given this called "Vision"
So far ahead of its time
I think it would have been better
If I never knew the promise until it was mine

Waiting for the time for dreams to manifest
Is not a time that is of anyone's best
To know, To see, To feel,
To even hear that which you know will be
Yet not be allowed to touch
To live . . . what you alone can see

This is more challenging than one would dare to dream
This is as hard as waiting to spend life's eternity with thee

Then my eyes were open, my ears could hear
To rehearse the "Vision" of the Promise,
Shapes me for what is near
My dreams give me confidence that drowns the possible fears

My dreams are my assurance of what I was told
The Promise would for sure one day unfold

The "Vision" as it was given to me is being worked out
All I have to do is continue to believe and not doubt

I must keep pushing towards the finishing of my dream
Never mind how things may look or seem
The Promise is promised even if I cannot see

In spite of the hindrances that causes me to want to scream
I will walk in the Promise as I do in my dreams

I will keep thanking you Lord
For the "Vision" that is not a dream

"In The Will-While-On The Wheel Of God"

Then I went down to the potter's house, and Behold, he wrought a work on the wheels.
Jeremiah 18:3

God's Will: The Good and perfect place of God
God's Wheel: The Ever moving Hand of God

In the Will of God I am always blessed
On the Wheel of God I seek his righteousness

In the Will of God is the safest place to be
On the Wheel of God I am broken
By the one who died to set me free

In the Will of God before the storm arise you are alarmed
On the Wheel of God the devil seeks to do you harm

In the Will of God you will always land with your feet on the ground
On the Wheel of God life will spin you around and land you upside
down

In the Will of God heaven's promise will unfold
On the Wheel of God you will encounter ordeals untold

In the Will of God I am heard even before I pray
On the Wheel of God His ears seems to be closed to what I say

In the Will of God I am sheltered from the rain
On the Wheel of God I am open to life's pain

In The Will-While-On The Wheel Of God

In the Will of God I can smile knowing troubles won't last always
On the Wheel of God troubles come and seem to stay

In the Will of God he prepares me to be heard
On the Wheel of God He polishes me with his Holy word

In the Will of God I am seen as God's shining light
On the Wheel of God my light is not always so bright

In the Will of God I shall never be afraid
On the Wheel of God doubt clouds my way

In the Will of God He gets all the Glory
On the Wheel of God He is writing my story

In the Will of God the Victory's already won
On the Wheel of God my end has just begun

In the Will of God I am On His Wheel
Ever growing, ever sowing, ever moving in Victory

The Cross-In The Middle

And he said unto Jesus, Lord, remember me
when thou comest into thy kingdom.
And Jesus said unto him,
Verily I say unto thee,
Today shalt thou be with me in paradise.
Luke 23:42-43

$\mathcal{T}$wo thieves One Savior
Bitter, Better and Redeemed

The thief on the left
Became Bitter due to the cross he bore
With his last breath he rebelled
Mocking and Denying Christ the Lord

The thief on the Right
Became Better due to the cross he bore
With his last breath, he defended the Lord
Only asking for a Mercy's reward

The Cross In The Middle
Bore our Lord as He bore his Cross
There He became Savior for ALL Who is Lost
As He showed mercy to the thief on the cross
From heaven, He gives that and more
To all who calls

From The Cross In The Middle
Comes Redemption
For those on the Right and on the Left
Come one come All
To The Cross In The Middle

Only He Can Make Your Bitterness Better
Forever . . . With Redemption
He came for our soul completion

He paid the ultimate price
So we can reap Eternal Paradise

"The Untold Story"

Whither shall I go from thy Spirit?
Or whither shall I flee from thy Presence?
If I say, Surely the darkness shall cover me;
Even the night shall be light about me.
Psalm 139: 7, 11

The untold story is what one dares not to say
My untold story has made me what I am today

My untold story is untold by me but seen from above
The untold story and all my members were hidden in his love

The things that you've done behind closed doors
Those things you know was rotten to the core
The master seen all yet you He called

How many times have you done just one thing . . .
That made you wish you would wake up and find it all a dream

Yes we've gone through hell
From the many things we failed
Then awakened crying from the nightmare
But in the midst of the darkness you learned of his loving care

The untold story will bring tears to your eyes
My untold story looking back even I am surprised
The hand of God carried me through
Even while I walked as a blinded fool

The things of my past is why Jesus' love is true
No one else could love me through the things I continued to do
With his mercy and tender hand
He gave me chance after chance and chance again . . .

Have you ever done just one thing that caused you open shame
You felt so bad you wished you could hide your face and change your
name
Yes, I too was shamed face
It humble me to receive his grace

Oh yes, some pretend to have never done anything wrong
Had it not been for God's mercy
You know you would now stand alone
Sentenced to HELL in this life and Eternal to Burn

The Untold Story

He stood beside you when no other did
Through your wrong His love He never hid

What is it that you have done to cause yourself great pain
The weight was so great it almost cause you to go in sane
But by God's love and His strength inside
Gave you hope to make it through that darkest night

Never forget the wrong you hide
Because of it you are more humble and not full of pride
The untold story is why you are who you are today
Never stop giving God His deserving praise

My untold story has caused me to never judge my sister or brother
My untold story has taught me none is perfect with faults we are no
different from another
My untold story has made me to know myself
My untold story is an open book on many shelves

But have my WHOLE Story EVER been told . . .?
Yes, to the Master only for He alone has the
POWER to HEAL my Soul

Go ahead don't be shame
The Mater know you are not all to blame
Release your story in the Master's care
He's waiting to hear only what He can bare

Your Story *Untold*
Will STOP you-from being Whole
With hidden darkness within your Soul

So all your cares do now bring
So you can spread your butterfly Wings
So the world can see the Love and the Light
Of Jesus our eternal Savior: The Christ

Fly Butterfly Fly
You have been set FREE